Amos

K.W. Bow

Copyright 2017 by Kenneth W. Bow
The book author retains sole copyright to
his contributions to this book.
Published 2017.
Printed in the United States of America.

All rights reserved.

No portion of this book may be reproduced, stored in a retrieval system, or transmitted in any form or by any means – electronic, mechanical, photocopy, recording, scanning, or other – except for brief quotations in critical reviews or articles, without the prior written permission of the author.

ISBN 978-1-946234-09-4

Front cover design by Mark Gauthier.

This book was published by BookCrafters,
Parker, Colorado.
bookcrafterscolorado@gmail.com

This book may be ordered from
www.bookcrafters.net and other online bookstores.

Foreword

Thank you reader, for selecting my book. There are many choices of books and we all have a limited window of time to read. I appreciate you purchasing my product. It is a humbling thing to know someone would choose to purchase, and then read your work. I do not take it as a small matter. By purchasing and reading a book, the reader and the author form a certain bond as they travel a road together for a short time. It is especially rewarding when the two agree on the content. It is my hope you can find inspiration and life challenges in the pages of this small booklet.

From the days of my high school years I have found the Bible fascinating. I have travelled to Israel on two occasions to learn more about the land and culture of the Bible. I worked on an archaeological dig and lived on a Kibbutz to better inform myself of how to understand this book from God. I have read it from cover to cover over twenty times, and it is still as exciting to me as it ever was.

The Bible is a magnificent journey and experience. It is ever a delight. In it you will travel to distant lands and meet some of the most incredible people of history. It will introduce you to kings and peasants. You will walk the palace halls of castles and the open fields of the countryside. You will meet the famous and be introduced to people whose name we will never know. You will read some of the greatest love stories ever told and you will see the dark side of man as the evil manifests itself in heinous ways. Every emotion of man is highlighted at some time. You will see greed and avarice and murderous covetousness. You will also see the greatest examples of love and sacrifice that mankind has ever contributed. For indeed the Bible is the story of man. It is the whole story, and nothing is left out or omitted. It is the ultimate mirror of life.

When we invest time in the Bible we indulge a bit of the eternal. The Bible will never pass away, even in the eons of the future. If you have read it sincerely then my hope is this small work will intensify your understanding and enjoyment a little more. It is the grandest journey we can make while in this life. Thank you for sharing a portion of your life journey with me.

Kenneth Bow

Introduction

Things had never been better. Israel was at the pinnacle of her national power. Trade and commerce were at an all time high. For the first time in many generations there was no threat of war. Merchants began to pile up profits. The people had luxuries they had only heard of. New homes were springing up everywhere. Beautiful ivory laid furniture was in the homes of the affluent. Meat, wine, body lotions were all common place in every home.

Then one lone voice rose above the din of pleasure. From the southern kingdom a lone prophet had come to town with a new message. Amos first two sermons ingratiated him with the rich elite socialites of Jerusalem. Everything was going well. Then, Amos' third sermon exploded their carefully constructed lives. Amos called these expensively coiffured socialites a bunch of cows. The priest challenged the Prophet and judgment fell quickly.

Amos was no professional prophet. He was a herdsman from lowly Tekoa in the south. He addressed a religious group of people who were regular church goers. They were comfortable and looking forward to the Day of the Lord. Suddenly a prophet was bringing bad news. God said,

"I hate, I despise your religious festivals." God wanted justice. Amos focuses on the injustice of Israelite society.

The rich were abusing the poor to get luxuries. They paraded their devotion to God like future Pharisees. They wanted God to fit neatly into their lives. Amos informed them God must be master over all of life, even business.

Amos was rough and unpolished. He did not fit in their cultured, opulent life style. His language is coarse and plain. His allusions are from the country. He speaks of baskets of fruit and plumb lines. The simplest person in society could understand his plain language. All men understand the language of cruelty and inhumanity. Amos predicted coming judgment. From the moment he spoke these words, Israel began to spiral downward. In the next thirteen years five Kings took the throne. Three were assassinated. Within thirty years Israel had been dismantled by Assyria.

Amos again illustrates that God used Prophets as His direct mouthpiece to the people because the priesthood had failed in its function.

Chapter 1

1.1-2 The words of Amos, who was among the herdmen of Tekoa, which he saw concerning Israel in the days of Uzziah king of Judah, and in the days of Jeroboam the son of Joash king of Israel, two years before the earthquake. 2 And he said, The Lord will roar from Zion, and utter his voice from Jerusalem; and the habitations of the shepherds shall mourn, and the top of Carmel shall wither.

1.1-2 Amos begins by documenting the moment of his prophecy according to a well known earthquake. This earthquake was also mentioned by Joel and Zechariah. It is a reminder of God's great power in nature.

1.3-5 Thus saith the Lord; For three transgressions of Damascus, and for four, I will not turn away the punishment thereof; because they have threshed Gilead with threshing instruments of iron: 4 But I will send a fire into the house of Hazael, which shall devour the palaces of Benhadad. 5 I will break also the bar of Damascus, and cut off the inhabitant from the plain of Aven, and him that holdeth the sceptre from the house of Eden: and the people of Syria shall go into captivity unto Kir, saith the Lord.

1.3-5 Damascus. This capital city of Syria had a long history of cruelty toward Jerusalem. This judgment brought great satisfaction to the Jewish populace of the Northern Kingdom. The phrase for three transgressions and for four is a rhetorical way of saying the offender is guilty of many offenses. The plain of Aven is an area where idolatry was deeply entrenched. The house of Eden (pleasure), probably has reference to the King of Syria's palace.

1.6-8 Thus saith the Lord; For three transgressions of Gaza, and for four, I will not turn away the punishment thereof; because they carried away captive the whole captivity, to deliver them up to Edom: 7 But I will send a fire on the wall of Gaza, which shall devour the palaces thereof: 8 And I will cut off the inhabitant from Ashdod, and him that holdeth the sceptre from Ashkelon, and I will turn mine hand against Ekron: and the remnant of the Philistines shall perish, saith the Lord God.

1.6-8 Gaza. This prophecy was a prophecy against Philistia as a whole, as it names several cities of that country. Philistia took the whole populace of Israel captive and delivered it to Edom. This is mentioned in Joel 3.3-8. The prophecy that Philistia will be cut off and perish has been fulfilled.

1.9-10 Thus saith the Lord; For three transgressions of Tyrus, and for four, I will not turn away the punishment thereof; because they delivered up the whole captivity to Edom, and remembered not the brotherly covenant: 10 But I will send a fire on the wall of Tyrus, which shall devour the palaces thereof.

1.9-10 Tyrus. Tyre did not remember the covenant that King Hiram made with David and Solomon. This agreement had been in place for many years and no King of Israel or Judah had ever warred on Phoenicia. Judah honored her side of the treaty but Phoenicia sold the people of Israel to others (Joel 3.4-8). God expects promises to be honored and kept.

1.11-12 Thus saith the Lord; For three transgressions of Edom, and for four, I will not turn away the punishment thereof; because he did pursue his brother with the sword, and did cast off all pity, and his anger did tear perpetually, and he kept his wrath for ever: 12 But I will send a fire upon Teman, which shall devour the palaces of Bozrah.

1.11-12 Edom. The judgment of Edom is enunciated clearly in the book of Obadiah. Edom pursued his brother Israel with the sword. One of David's most admired qualities was he never lifted a sword against another Israeli. To fight and betray a brother is a cause of great angst in the heart of God.

1.13-15 Thus saith the Lord; For three transgressions of the children of Ammon, and for four, I will not turn away the punishment thereof; because they have ripped up the women with child of Gilead, that they might enlarge their border: 14 But I will kindle a fire in the wall of Rabbah, and it shall devour the palaces thereof, with shouting in the day of battle, with a tempest in the day of the whirlwind: 15 And their king shall go into captivity, he and his princes together, saith the Lord.

1.13-15 Ammon. Long an enemy of Israel and Judah, Amos asserts this evil and wicked nation will meet it's demise for it's unspeakable atrocities against God's people. Beginning in the time of the Judges, through the wars of Hazael the King of Syria, and Sihon the King of the Amorites, the nation of Ammon had ripped up women with child and committed unspeakable cruelties. As punishment their capital was to be burned, the nation put in exile, and their kingdom destroyed. The message of this chapter is clear: God keeps records and will bring every work into judgment.

Chapter 2

2.1-3 Thus saith the Lord; For three transgressions of Moab, and for four, I will not turn away the punishment thereof; because he burned the bones of the king of Edom into lime: 2 But I will send a fire upon Moab, and it shall devour the palaces of Kirioth: and Moab shall die with tumult, with shouting, and with the sound of the trumpet: 3 And I will cut off the judge from the midst thereof, and will slay all the princes thereof with him, saith the Lord.

2.1-3 Moab. The genesis of Moab was the same as Ammon (Lot's daughters), and the result was much the same also. Interesting the view of God; the burning of bones of the King of Edom. God's judgment is reserved usually for actions toward His people. If this holds true, this would refer to the time Edom was a vassal of Israel after the war involving Joram and Jehoshaphat against Moab. The Moabites dug up the bones of the King of Edom and burned them to add insult to injury. If this is indeed the reference of the prophet, then it clearly shows God is also concerned about the peripheral issues of His people also.

2.4-5 Thus saith the Lord; For three transgressions of Judah, and for four, I will not turn away the punishment

thereof; because they have despised the law of the Lord, and have not kept his commandments, and their lies caused them to err, after the which their fathers have walked: 5 But I will send a fire upon Judah, and it shall devour the palaces of Jerusalem.

2.4-5 Judah. This is one of the sermons that ingratiated Amos to the socialites of the Northern Kingdom. The long simmering issues with the Southern Nation of Judah were ongoing. To hear a judgment against Judah made these Israelites rejoice and feel smug. Little did they know their sermon was coming soon. Both Israel and Judah had violated the law of God and were equally on God's radar. Both nations were on a countdown to destruction.

2.6-16 Thus saith the Lord; For three transgressions of Israel, and for four, I will not turn away the punishment thereof; because they sold the righteous for silver, and the poor for a pair of shoes; 7 That pant after the dust of the earth on the head of the poor, and turn aside the way of the meek: and a man and his father will go in unto the same maid, to profane my holy name: 8 And they lay themselves down upon clothes laid to pledge by every altar, and they drink the wine of the condemned in the house of their god. 9 Yet destroyed I the Amorite before them, whose height was like the height of the cedars, and he was strong as the oaks; yet I destroyed his fruit from above, and his roots from beneath. 10 Also I brought you up from the land of Egypt, and led you forty years through the wilderness, to possess the land of the Amorite. 11 And I raised up of your sons for prophets, and of your young men for Nazarites. Is it not even thus, O ye children of Israel? saith the Lord. 12 But ye gave the Nazarites wine to drink; and commanded the prophets, saying, Prophesy not. 13 Behold, I am pressed

under you, as a cart is pressed that is full of sheaves. 14 Therefore the flight shall perish from the swift, and the strong shall not strengthen his force, neither shall the mighty deliver himself: 15 Neither shall he stand that handleth the bow; and he that is swift of foot shall not deliver himself: neither shall he that rideth the horse deliver himself. 16 And he that is courageous among the mighty shall flee away naked in that day, saith the Lord.

2.6-16 Israel. The joy of judgment on Judah was short lived, for in the next breath, Amos prophecies about Israel. The list of grievous issues is long and detailed. As Amos lists the flagrant violations of God's law, the heart of the people sank lower and lower. God had reached His breaking point with this Northern Kingdom. The sins of selling out the righteous for money, ignoring the meek (God's choice in people), sexual impurity, drinking the wine of the condemned, all in juxtaposition to God destroying their enemies, bringing them out of Egypt, raising their sons to be prophets, finally caused God to feel like He was pressed under a cart full of sheaves. The clock had ticked down to the final moment and judgment had arrived. Amos was the voice announcing that moment. There was to be no escape nor deliverance. Omnibus rebus bonis finis est, for all good things there is an end.

Chapter 3

3.1-3 Hear this word that the Lord hath spoken against you, O children of Israel, against the whole family which I brought up from the land of Egypt, saying, 2 You only have I known of all the families of the earth: therefore I will punish you for all your iniquities. 3 Can two walk together, except they be agreed?

3.1-3 You only have I known. This is one of the most endearing statements God ever made to Israel. The Hebrew word *yada* is a broad term. It has the connotation of knowing in many ways. It speaks of God taking time and care to truly "know" the nation of Israel above all nations of the earth (Ez 20.5). God revealed himself and extended himself to Israel and Israel's response was indifference, and now the great God of heaven feels all the feelings of a jilted lover. God cannot walk with Israel unless they both reciprocate. God chose Israel out of all the peoples of the earth, and her response was to be unfaithful.

3.4-8 Will a lion roar in the forest, when he hath no prey? will a young lion cry out of his den, if he have taken nothing? 5 Can a bird fall in a snare upon the earth, where no gin is for him? shall one take up a snare from the earth, and have taken nothing at all? 6 Shall a trumpet

be blown in the city, and the people not be afraid? shall there be evil in a city, and the Lord hath not done it? 7 Surely the Lord God will do nothing, but he revealeth his secret unto his servants the prophets. 8 The lion hath roared, who will not fear? the Lord God hath spoken, who can but prophesy?

3.4-8 The yearnings of God. God is speaking like a lion roars or a bird caught in a snare. There is cause for His complaint. The voice of Amos is God crying out to the nation, please listen to me. Israel did not see the future of the next three decades but God did, and the future was bleak for this backslid nation.

3.9-15 Publish in the palaces at Ashdod, and in the palaces in the land of Egypt, and say, Assemble yourselves upon the mountains of Samaria, and behold the great tumults in the midst thereof, and the oppressed in the midst thereof. 10 For they know not to do right, saith the Lord, who store up violence and robbery in their palaces. 11 Therefore thus saith the Lord God; An adversary there shall be even round about the land; and he shall bring down thy strength from thee, and thy palaces shall be spoiled. 12 Thus saith the Lord; As the shepherd taketh out of the mouth of the lion two legs, or a piece of an ear; so shall the children of Israel be taken out that dwell in Samaria in the corner of a bed, and in Damascus in a couch. 13 Hear ye, and testify in the house of Jacob, saith the Lord God, the God of hosts, 14 That in the day that I shall visit the transgressions of Israel upon him I will also visit the altars of Bethel: and the horns of the altar shall be cut off, and fall to the ground. 15 And I will smite the winter house with the summer house; and the houses of ivory shall perish, and the great houses shall have an end, saith the Lord.

3.9-15. The mind of the country preacher presents a vivid unforgettable image in this passage. The image of a nation torn in pieces by powerful nations around them. As a lover, God had held off these nations from invading Israel, but now He announces these nations will be free to plunder and ravage Israel. When these nations have satiated their unholy lust on God's people the final result will be like a shepherd who finds only pieces of an attacked and torn animal. There will only be two legs or a piece of an ear, so shall the children of Israel be taken. God as a jilted lover responds with lifting His protection and Egypt and Damascus are loosed on weak defenseless Israel. Israel never got the revelation that God was their refuge and strength. As a final coup de grace, God announces their houses of Ivory shall perish. All of their pride and accumulated possessions will be plundered by Philistia and Egypt.

Chapter 4

4.1-5 Hear this word, ye kine of Bashan, that are in the mountain of Samaria, which oppress the poor, which crush the needy, which say to their masters, Bring, and let us drink. 2 The Lord God hath sworn by his holiness, that, lo, the days shall come upon you, that he will take you away with hooks, and your posterity with fishhooks. 3 And ye shall go out at the breaches, every cow at that which is before her; and ye shall cast them into the palace, saith the Lord. 4 Come to Bethel, and transgress; at Gilgal multiply transgression; and bring your sacrifices every morning, and your tithes after three years: 5 And offer a sacrifice of thanksgiving with leaven, and proclaim and publish the free offerings: for this liketh you, O ye children of Israel, saith the Lord God.

4.1-5 The indictment. Amos begins to list the travesties of Israel. Amos uses strong language by calling them Kine (cows). The cows of Bashan were well fed and strong because of the lush vegetation of the area. This is much more than an insult in itself. The illustration is a full grown cow leading her calves. This is not just about the Israel of now, but for many years the offspring will be led into captivity. These cows have oppressed the poor and gotten fat off the reward of their mistreatment of the poor.

So the prophet mocks them with his words; come to Bethel and transgress, to Gilgal and multiply transgression. He continues to mock them by saying offer a sacrifice of thanksgiving with leaven. This is an apt reference to all their sacrifices being polluted.

4.6-13 And I also have given you cleanness of teeth in all your cities, and want of bread in all your places: yet have ye not returned unto me, saith the Lord. 7 And also I have withholden the rain from you, when there were yet three months to the harvest: and I caused it to rain upon one city, and caused it not to rain upon another city: one piece was rained upon, and the piece whereupon it rained not withered. 8 So two or three cities wandered unto one city, to drink water; but they were not satisfied: yet have ye not returned unto me, saith the Lord. 9 I have smitten you with blasting and mildew: when your gardens and your vineyards and your fig trees and your olive trees increased, the palmerworm devoured them: yet have ye not returned unto me, saith the Lord. 10 I have sent among you the pestilence after the manner of Egypt: your young men have I slain with the sword, and have taken away your horses; and I have made the stink of your camps to come up unto your nostrils: yet have ye not returned unto me, saith the Lord. 11 I have overthrown some of you, as God overthrew Sodom and Gomorrah, and ye were as a firebrand plucked out of the burning: yet have ye not returned unto me, saith the Lord. 12 Therefore thus will I do unto thee, O Israel: and because I will do this unto thee, prepare to meet thy God, O Israel. 13 For, lo, he that formeth the mountains, and createth the wind, and declareth unto man what is his thought, that maketh the morning darkness, and treadeth upon the high places of the earth, The Lord, The God of hosts, is his name.

4.6-13 God's defense. God is always fair. Here Amos presents his defense of God and God's long suffering. God tried. God sent cleanness of teeth (famine), want of bread (poor crops), drought (no rain), God even selected cities to rain on and not to rain on another, but Israel just did not get the message. The voice from God the jilted lover said, yet have ye not returned unto me, saith the Lord. God then went further in trying to get through to his beloved people. God sent blasting and mildew, the worms destroyed their crops, pestilence and war, until life literally stunk in their nostrils, and still Israel never made the turn to her God. God gave a sample of the judgment to come by overthrowing some of them like Sodom and then plucking them out of danger just in the nick of time. Nothing in all of this impacted this people that God loved so much. A frustrated God now announces: prepare to meet thy God. He that formed mountains and creates the wind, the all powerful God who has loved such fallen mankind, has reached the end of His patience with a disobedient nation. With a formal declaration of His name He steps back and allows judgment to descend on Israel.

Chapter 5

5.1-3 Hear ye this word which I take up against you, even a lamentation, O house of Israel. 2 The virgin of Israel is fallen; she shall no more rise: she is forsaken upon her land; there is none to raise her up. 3 For thus saith the Lord God; The city that went out by a thousand shall leave an hundred, and that which went forth by an hundred shall leave ten, to the house of Israel.

5.1-3 The verdict is in, the sentence is passed, the virgin of Israel is fallen. Israel is decimated. The spiritual forecast is, one tenth shall survive. Thus Amos laments the moment.

5.4-6 For thus saith the Lord unto the house of Israel, Seek ye me, and ye shall live: 5 But seek not Bethel, nor enter into Gilgal, and pass not to Beersheba: for Gilgal shall surely go into captivity, and Bethel shall come to nought. 6 Seek the Lord, and ye shall live; lest he break out like fire in the house of Joseph, and devour it, and there be none to quench it in Bethel.

5.4-6 Even at this precipitous moment, still the strain of mercy bleeds through. Three times the invitation is given seek ye me and ye shall live. Judgment can be postponed or avoided. The only hope at this point is to seek the Lord.

God jettisons their religious places like Bethel, Gilgal or Beersheba. These places had rich pasts but had ceased to point the people to God. The admonition is to seek God, not their past moments of religion. This is the trap of all religious experiences of God. The quest to keep our devotions as fresh manna every day is our daily challenge. This is mirrored in the Lord's prayer, give us this day our daily bread.

5.7-10 Ye who turn judgment to wormwood, and leave off righteousness in the earth, 8 Seek him that maketh the seven stars and Orion, and turneth the shadow of death into the morning, and maketh the day dark with night: that calleth for the waters of the sea, and poureth them out upon the face of the earth: The Lord is his name: 9 That strengtheneth the spoiled against the strong, so that the spoiled shall come against the fortress. 10 They hate him that rebuketh in the gate, and they abhor him that speaketh uprightly.

5.7-10 These people were religious. The judgment from God came because their religion was self serving. Judgment and righteousness were not offered to God, but rather used as a medium to reach their own selfish ends. Religion of itself is not always pleasing to God. Religion must exalt God and point men to God to be efficacious. Those who practice self serving religion hate those who speak uprightly.

5.11-17 Forasmuch therefore as your treading is upon the poor, and ye take from him burdens of wheat: ye have built houses of hewn stone, but ye shall not dwell in them; ye have planted pleasant vineyards, but ye shall not drink wine of them. 12 For I know your manifold transgressions and your mighty sins: they afflict the just,

they take a bribe, and they turn aside the poor in the gate from their right. 13 Therefore the prudent shall keep silence in that time; for it is an evil time. 14 Seek good, and not evil, that ye may live: and so the Lord, the God of hosts, shall be with you, as ye have spoken. 15 Hate the evil, and love the good, and establish judgment in the gate: it may be that the Lord God of hosts will be gracious unto the remnant of Joseph. 16 Therefore the Lord, the God of hosts, the Lord, saith thus; Wailing shall be in all streets; and they shall say in all the highways, Alas! alas! and they shall call the husbandman to mourning, and such as are skilful of lamentation to wailing. 17 And in all vineyards shall be wailing: for I will pass through thee, saith the Lord.

5.11-17 Many people associate religion with a church or synagogue. God never intended anyone to have "church house" religion. One man said if your religion does not work at home it does not work, so do not export it. This passage shows how Israel's self serving religion did not accomplish the purpose of true religion. This is what brought God to the end of His patience and invoked judgment. God will not share His glory with another. Mistreatment of the poor, the manifold transgressions of their mighty sins, afflicting the just, was no longer to be tolerated. The call from God was to choose between good and evil, and establish judgment in the gate. As a result of their selfish, self centered, religion, they would wail and mourn in the same streets where they had ravaged and mistreated the poor. This travail would spill out of the city and into the countryside and vineyards.

5.18-27 Woe unto you that desire the day of the Lord! to what end is it for you? the day of the Lord is darkness, and not light. 19 As if a man did flee from a lion, and a bear met him; or went into the house, and leaned his hand on the wall, and a serpent bit him. 20 Shall not the day of the Lord be darkness, and not light? even very dark, and no brightness in it? 21 I hate, I despise your feast days, and I will not smell in your solemn assemblies. 22 Though ye offer me burnt offerings and your meat offerings, I will not accept them: neither will I regard the peace offerings of your fat beasts. 23 Take thou away from me the noise of thy songs; for I will not hear the melody of thy viols. 24 But let judgment run down as waters, and righteousness as a mighty stream. 25 Have ye offered unto me sacrifices and offerings in the wilderness forty years, O house of Israel? 26 But ye have borne the tabernacle of your Moloch and Chiun your images, the star of your god, which ye made to yourselves. 27 Therefore will I cause you to go into captivity beyond Damascus, saith the Lord, whose name is The God of hosts.

5.18-27 These quasi-religious people had loudly proclaimed their desire for the Day of the Lord. Now it was coming and God proclaims it will not be to your liking. They are informed they will not escape. It will be darkness, and liken to fleeing from wild beasts. Why? Because God came to despise their feast days. This was because their religion was all about "them". God was not part of the true purpose of what they did under the guise of religion. They offered their burnt offerings and meat offerings and God said no thanks. God sadly declares he does not want to hear their songs. God is looking for righteousness, not hypocrisy. The years of accumulated offerings that these people thought were pleasing to God, are rejected by God wholesale. The indictment includes their inclusion of Moloch and Chiun (Hebrew kiyun~idol), in their worship. The cup of God's anger and disgust is full. The gavel in the hand of God falls and the words hang in the air pregnant with fear, "Therefore will I cause you to go into captivity". From beautiful homes, ivory furniture, wealth and opulence, body oils and luxury, and comfortable well organized religion, to captivity in one fell swoop. How are the mighty brought low.

Chapter 6

6.1-6 Woe to them that are at ease in Zion, and trust in the mountain of Samaria, which are named chief of the nations, to whom the house of Israel came! 2 Pass ye unto Calneh, and see; and from thence go ye to Hamath the great: then go down to Gath of the Philistines: be they better than these kingdoms? or their border greater than your border? 3 Ye that put far away the evil day, and cause the seat of violence to come near; 4 That lie upon beds of ivory, and stretch themselves upon their couches, and eat the lambs out of the flock, and the calves out of the midst of the stall; 5 That chant to the sound of the viol, and invent to themselves instruments of musick, like David; 6 That drink wine in bowls, and anoint themselves with the chief ointments: but they are not grieved for the affliction of Joseph.

6.1-6 Ease is always the desire of man. The use of the Hebrew word (shaanan) here has to do with being secure. Amos let them know they think they are secure and have life lined up perfectly. These people had put the evil day far into the future and out of their mind. They were laying upon beds of ivory and eating rich food without a care in the world. Everything was perfectly in order. They chanted to the sound of the viol like David, meaning their music was the best. David's music was inspired by God and brought people into fellowship with God, whereas this music was excellent and flawless, but was sensual and carnal. God was not a part of their music. They were in their bathes and using their oils while unconcerned about the world around them. This attitude is similar to the well known refrain "Nero fiddled while Rome burned". They were so sated by opulence they were unaware their world was crashing down around them. The reason? The affliction of Joseph (can also mean adding). These socialites had continued to add more and more selfish misuse on the poor. The result? The result was to be captivity.

6.7-14 Therefore now shall they go captive with the first that go captive, and the banquet of them that stretched themselves shall be removed. 8 The Lord God hath sworn by himself, saith the Lord the God of hosts, I abhor the excellency of Jacob, and hate his palaces: therefore will I deliver up the city with all that is therein. 9 And it shall come to pass, if there remain ten men in one house, that they shall die. 10 And a man's uncle shall take him up, and he that burneth him, to bring out the bones out of the house, and shall say unto him that is by the sides of the house, Is there yet any with thee? and he shall say, No. Then shall he say, Hold thy tongue: for we may not make mention of the name of the Lord. 11 For, behold, the Lord commandeth, and he will smite the great house with breaches, and the little house with clefts. 12 Shall horses run upon the rock? will one plow there with oxen? for ye have turned judgment into gall, and the fruit of righteousness into hemlock: 13 Ye which rejoice in a thing of nought, which say, Have we not taken to us horns by our own strength? 14 But, behold, I will raise up against you a nation, O house of Israel, saith the

Lord the God of hosts; and they shall afflict you from the entering in of Hemath unto the river of the wilderness.

6.7-14 The captivity. The Lord continues to present His case against these pseudo-religious socialites. God documents His case completely. God abhors the excellency (arrogancy), of Jacob. Pride is always a stink in the nostrils of God, and never more so than at this moment. God delivers the entire city to destruction. A man's uncle (hebrew~dod), lover, friend, family member, will betray them to the captors. Every house will fall, the great houses and also the small houses. God's anger is all consuming. Amos the country preacher illustrates with metaphors from his rural life. Shall horses run upon the rock? He illustrates the judgment, or verdict, has been turned into poison. The promise from God is a nation is coming that will afflict you from Syria to Egypt. These wealthy patrons of ease had trusted in their own resources and now their resources will not suffice to deliver them. Riches never deliver in the day of death and judgment.

Chapter 7

7.1-3 Thus hath the Lord God shewed unto me; and, behold, he formed grasshoppers in the beginning of the shooting up of the latter growth; and, lo, it was the latter growth after the king's mowings. 2 And it came to pass, that when they had made an end of eating the grass of the land, then I said, O Lord God, forgive, I beseech thee: by whom shall Jacob arise? for he is small. 3 The Lord repented for this: It shall not be, saith the Lord.

7.1-3 Grasshoppers. God allowed them to plant the crop, water the crop, even cut the mowing so their hopes were strong for a good harvest, then sent the locusts to devour their labor and profit. The question arises; was God deliberately letting them hope before destroying their hopes? Was God delaying the judgment in hopes they would come to their senses? Acts 15.18 lets us know, known unto God are all His works from the beginning of the world. It would seem God foreknew they would not change and repent so He allowed them to go through all the planning, all the labor, and all the expectation before dashing their hopes. God wants to imprint the lesson firmly into their minds that He alone controls all of nature and by extension all their lives. Locusts seem to be a particular choice of judgment from God. This may date all the way back to the creation of Adam and his creation from the soil. Locusts lie dormant in the soil until such a time God summons them to His purpose. From the soil God can summon life, man or judgment.

7.4-6 Thus hath the Lord God shewed unto me: and, behold, the Lord God called to contend by fire, and it devoured the great deep, and did eat up a part. 5 Then said I, O Lord God, cease, I beseech thee: by whom shall Jacob arise? for he is small. 6 The Lord repented for this: This also shall not be, saith the Lord God.

7.4-6 Fire. Fire is a major symbol of judgment. In 1.4 God had said He would send fire as judgment on the house of Hazael. We know in the final chapters of life on earth, fire is a major factor. Hell and the lake of fire are reserved for the Devil and the beast and the false prophet. Fire is reserved for all who do not obey the gospel of Jesus Christ. The fire summoned here is not a small blaze for it devours the great deep. A fire powerful enough to destroy the oceans of the world seems inconceivable to our mind. Yet this is what Amos announces will happen.

7.7-9 Thus he shewed me: and, behold, the Lord stood upon a wall made by a plumbline, with a plumbline in his hand. And the Lord said unto me, Amos, what seest thou? And I said, A plumbline. Then said the Lord, Behold, I will set a plumbline in the midst of my people Israel: I will not again pass by them any more: 9 And the high places of Isaac shall be desolate, and the sanctuaries of Israel shall be laid waste; and I will rise against the house of Jeroboam with the sword.

7.7-9 Plumbline. The wall was the nation and people of Israel. When the righteous line of God was held against this wall, the wall showed how far the nation was off course. Their vision of themselves could not see the drift. By holding the plumbline against the wall, the drift was stark and the nation was without excuse. The drift was undeniable. The nation was far from where they once were. Spiritual drift is difficult to measure. The gradual nature of drift is so subtle it is hard to perceive. God wanted the nation to see how far they had moved from their beginnings. The house of Jeroboam was to be removed forever. This happened when Assyria invaded in 721 BC and carried away 200,000 captives. The northern country, here called the house of Jeroboam, exits the stage forever.

7.10-13 Then Amaziah the priest of Bethel sent to Jeroboam king of Israel, saying, Amos hath conspired against thee in the midst of the house of Israel: the land is not able to bear all his words. 11 For thus Amos saith, Jeroboam shall die by the sword, and Israel shall surely be led away captive out of their own land. 12 Also Amaziah said unto Amos, O thou seer, go, flee thee away into the land of Judah, and there eat bread, and prophesy there: 13 But prophesy not again any more at Bethel: for it is the king's chapel, and it is the king's court.

7.10-13 Amaziah's treachery. Now comes a shift in the line of Amos' visions of judgment to describe a parenthetical moment. Amaziah, the high priest of this self sufficient religious people, resented the ministry of Amos. Amos was dismantling the High Priest's playhouse of insincere religion. The high priest strikes back by accusing Amos of treason and demands the prophet go home and leave them alone. This is a false accusation and draws an immediate reaction from Amos, and an immediate judgment form God.

7.14-17 Then answered Amos, and said to Amaziah, I was no prophet, neither was I a prophet's son; but I was an herdman, and a gatherer of sycomore fruit: 15 And the Lord took me as I followed the flock, and the Lord said unto me, Go, prophesy unto my people Israel. 16 Now therefore hear thou the word of the Lord: Thou sayest, Prophesy not against Israel, and drop not thy word against the house of Isaac. 17 Therefore thus saith the Lord; Thy wife shall be an harlot in the city, and thy sons and thy daughters shall fall by the sword, and thy land shall be divided by line; and thou shalt die in a polluted land: and Israel shall surely go into captivity forth of his land.

7.14-17 Amaziah's judgment. This judgment is a minuscule view of the larger picture of Israel rejecting the voice of the prophets all the way back to Samuel. Amos declares he did not ask for this job. He was a lowly shepherd doing the most menial job in the country (gathering sycamore fruit). He was not the son of a prophet, and therefore an unlikely candidate to pronounce judgment upon an entire nation. God called this uneducated, rough hewn prophet to show His power and glory and veracity are not always found in the esteemed of men. God chose the basest of men to pronounce judgment on the nation, when the nation was at the zenith of power and wealth and influence. Like a lash, the words of Amos flick out and sting the high priest. The high priest is informed his wife will be a harlot and his children will die by the sword. Amaziah will perish, as all will, who resist the word of a God called man. This moment, frozen in time, illustrates God's principal of vengeance. God declares in Rom 12.19, vengeance is mine, I will repay. The message was loud and clear. Raise your voice against this prophecy, resist this prophecy, and there will be swift and harsh judgment.

Chapter 8

8.1-14 Thus hath the Lord God shewed unto me: and behold a basket of summer fruit. 2 And he said, Amos, what seest thou? And I said, A basket of summer fruit. Then said the Lord unto me, The end is come upon my people of Israel; I will not again pass by them any more. 3 And the songs of the temple shall be howlings in that day, saith the Lord God: there shall be many dead bodies in every place; they shall cast them forth with silence. 4 Hear this, O ye that swallow up the needy, even to make the poor of the land to fail, 5 Saying, When will the new moon be gone, that we may sell corn? and the sabbath, that we may set forth wheat, making the ephah small, and the shekel great, and falsifying the balances by deceit? 6 That we may buy the poor for silver, and the needy for a pair of shoes; yea, and sell the refuse of the wheat? 7 The Lord hath sworn by the excellency of Jacob, Surely I will never forget any of their works. 8 Shall not the land tremble for this, and every one mourn that dwelleth therein? and it shall rise up wholly as a flood; and it shall be cast out and drowned, as by the flood of Egypt. 9 And it shall come to pass in that day, saith the Lord God, that I will cause the sun to go down at noon, and I will darken the earth in the clear day: 10 And I will turn your feasts into mourning, and all your songs into lamentation; and I will bring up sackcloth upon all loins, and baldness upon every head; and I will make it as the mourning of an only son, and the end thereof as a bitter day. 11 Behold, the days come, saith the Lord God, that I will send a famine in the land, not a famine of bread, nor a thirst for water, but of hearing the words of the Lord: 12 And they shall wander from sea to sea, and from the north even to the east, they shall run to and fro to seek the word of the Lord, and shall not find it. 13 In that day shall the fair virgins and young men faint for thirst. 14 They that swear by the sin of Samaria, and say, Thy god, O Dan, liveth; and, The manner of Beersheba liveth; even they shall fall, and never rise up again.

8.1-14 The summerfruit. In no other vision is the transparency of Amos seen like in this vision. This is purely the mind of a country boy frustrated by not being able to make these socialites see what is coming down the pike. Flailing desperately to make them understand, he grabs what should be the most simple illustration anyone could ask for. He shows them a basket of summer fruit. The fruit is over ripe. To his simple rustic mind even the most stubborn prejudiced mind could easily see the analogy. The basket of fruit represents this nation who is well past judgment. Decay is so obvious it smells. The fruit is soft and rotting. Amos patiently begins to explain. The temple will be filled with howling. There will be no deliverance there. Their crops will not buy them deliverance. Their injustice to the poor has finally rotted their mercy from God. Judgment will come as a flood. Their feasts will be turned into mourning, their songs into sad laments, poverty will overcome them, famine and drought are coming. The populace will be turned out to wander the world and never find God again. The funeral dirge of Samaria is being written and is about to be sung. The nation began by Jeroboam 200 years ago is now reduced to a basket of rotting fruit. No one in the world will ever desire to partake of this fruit again.

Chapter 9

9.1-10 I saw the Lord standing upon the altar: and he said, Smite the lintel of the door, that the posts may shake: and cut them in the head, all of them; and I will slay the last of them with the sword: he that fleeth of them shall not flee away, and he that escapeth of them shall not be delivered. 2 Though they dig into hell, thence shall mine hand take them; though they climb up to heaven, thence will I bring them down: 3 And though they hide themselves in the top of Carmel, I will search and take them out thence; and though they be hid from my sight in the bottom of the sea, thence will I command the serpent, and he shall bite them: 4 And though they go into captivity before their enemies, thence will I command the sword, and it shall slay them: and I will set mine eyes upon them for evil, and not for good. 5 And the Lord God of hosts is he that toucheth the land, and it shall melt, and all that dwell therein shall mourn: and it shall rise up wholly like a flood; and shall be drowned, as by the flood of Egypt. 6 It is he that buildeth his stories in the heaven, and hath founded his troop in the earth; he that calleth for the waters of the sea, and poureth them out upon the face of the earth: The Lord is his name. 7 Are ye not as children of the Ethiopians unto me, O children of

Israel? saith the Lord. Have not I brought up Israel out of the land of Egypt? and the Philistines from Caphtor, and the Syrians from Kir? 8 Behold, the eyes of the Lord God are upon the sinful kingdom, and I will destroy it from off the face of the earth; saving that I will not utterly destroy the house of Jacob, saith the Lord. 9 For, lo, I will command, and I will sift the house of Israel among all nations, like as corn is sifted in a sieve, yet shall not the least grain fall upon the earth. 10 All the sinners of my people shall die by the sword, which say, The evil shall not overtake nor prevent us.

9.1-10 The destruction of Israel. This is the final vision of Amos' prophecy recorded. It is assumed he returns to the south and lives out his life having delivered the coup de grace to a proud, defiant, unrepentant nation. Who can know his inner thoughts? Was he empty? Did he feel he accomplished his task? As with so many of the servants of God we have no insight to their inner feelings. We cannot know if he felt fulfilled or frustrated. Was he delighted or defeated? We cannot know. He sees the final vision here. He sees the Lord standing upon the altar. This is God's altar and He has come to claim ownership. God himself steps up on the altar and begins to dismantle the ugly pseudo-religion the nation has created. God announces there is no place to hide. From the depth of hell to the top of Carmel the searching eye of God will find them. Neither the depth of the sea or captivity in a foreign nation will provide sanctuary from God. Standing on the altar God proclaims his power and authority in heaven, in earth and in the seas. God sternly tells this backslid nation they are like Ethiopians to Him. God himself brought them into existence and He will take them out of existence as well. The heavenly sifting has begun. It is time for Amos to put down his writing instrument and go back to picking sycamore fruit. As the words die from Amos' lips, the sinners die from Samaria.

9.11-15 In that day will I raise up the tabernacle of David that is fallen, and close up the breaches thereof; and I will raise up his ruins, and I will build it as in the days of old: 12 That they may possess the remnant of Edom, and of all the heathen, which are called by my name, saith the Lord that doeth this. 13 Behold, the days come, saith the Lord, that the plowman shall overtake the reaper, and the treader of grapes him that soweth seed; and the mountains shall drop sweet wine, and all the hills shall melt. 14 And I will bring again the captivity of my people of Israel, and they shall build the waste cities, and inhabit them; and they shall plant vineyards, and drink the wine thereof; they shall also make gardens, and eat the fruit of them. 15 And I will plant them upon their land, and they shall no more be pulled up out of their land which I have given them, saith the Lord thy God.

9.11-15 The restoration. The rising of the sun every day mirrors God's mercy and grace. The sunset of God's mercy is yet to be viewed again in the sunrise of a future remnant. From these very ruins God will build the Tabernacle of David. James confirms this is the New Testament church, in the book of Acts when the counsel gathers to discuss the inclusion of Gentiles into the church. James has the spiritual sight to see through the smoke and haze of Israel's failure and see the Lord standing on that altar centuries before. At that momentous event in Acts chapter 15, James proclaims God has built again the Tabernacle of David. As dying leaves and humus give the earth the nutrients for new growth, so the death of the Northern Kingdom gave birth to the church. The church possesses the remnant of

Edom and all the heathen, which are called by the name of the Lord. The plowman over takes the reaper, and the treader of grapes him that soweth seed. The captivity of Israel is restored, cities are rebuilt, vineyards are planted, and gardens flourish. God closes this prophetical refrain by proclaiming He will plant them upon their land and they shall no more be pulled up. As the fading sunlight descends and Amos sees its final rays, he knows the sun will yet rise again. It shall rise in the glorious light of the Gospel and the whole earth shall be filled with it's glory.

The Story Behind the Expository Series

This is a story about a man, his morals, and his ethics. The man's name was Millard Deramus. He was my paternal grandfather.

Millard lived at the end of a dirt and gravel road in Western Central Arkansas. When the road, as it was, reached his homestead, it turned and headed out of the woods. He was born a quarter of a mile from where he lived his entire life. I am not sure if he ever ventured out of the state of Arkansas. Possibly he got as far as a neighboring state once.

Many years ago he had a neighbor he simply referred to as Mr. Poole. One day Mr. Poole left. When it came time to pay the yearly taxes on their property, Mr. Poole had not returned. Millard was a good neighbor, so he did what he felt good neighbors do, he decided Mr. Poole's taxes should be paid so when Mr. Poole returned, he would not be in arrears with the state of Arkansas.

Millard hitched his mules and went on to Mr. Poole's land and cut a load of pulp wood and took it to the mill and sold it. He then went to the county seat and paid Mr. Poole's taxes. The next year Mr. Poole had still not returned, so Millard again cut pulp wood off Mr. Poole's land, sold it, and paid the taxes on Mr. Poole's land. This continued for many, many years. Mr. Poole never returned and each year my grandfather would cut timber off of Mr. Poole's land and sell it and pay the taxes on Mr. Poole's land.

I was there the day the attorney came to see Millard. We were on the back porch that had been screened in, and we were drinking coffee. I still have the two coffee cups we used that day. I heard the conversation from three feet away. The attorney had a briefcase full of papers he wanted Millard to sign.

The attorney informed Millard that according to the state of Arkansas, Millard was the owner of the 280 acres next door by the default of paying the taxes for the last 20 years. The name Millard Deramus was on every yearly receipt for over 20 years. The amount of money being discussed was substantial. I watched my grandfather closely. There was no reaction at all. No smile, not even a raised eyebrow.

Millard patiently waited for the attorney to finish. The attorney requested my grandfather sign the documents accepting ownership of 280 acres that joined his 70 acres. The value of the land at that time, including the timber, was well over a quarter of a million dollars. When the attorney finished and asked my grandfather to sign the documents he quietly and firmly said no, I will not sign. He informed the attorney that was not his land and he had never taken anything that did not belong to him in his life.

The amount of money was staggering to me. I was watching a man who had lived a simple rustic life for all of his eighty-plus years. He wore bib overalls and drove old pick-up trucks. When younger, he worked as a blacksmith out under the oak tree in his yard. I still have items he forged under that old oak tree. I watched that day as the attorney attempted to stoke the fire of avarice in Millard Deramus.

The attorney told Millard all he could do with several hundred thousand dollars. He floated the idea of a new home, a new truck, retirement, travel. Millard just stared at the attorney. No comment. None. The attorney tried again. Will you just sign, Millard? For your children? No comment. None. Finally the attorney asked, "Is there anything I can do to get you to sign these papers?" My grandfather simply shook his head no. He said one sentence. He said, "It ain't my land."

My grandfather died and was buried a short distance from where he lived his entire life. My grandmother (Dolly) lived a few more years. The children convinced her to sign the papers to claim ownership of the land because otherwise it would simply go back to the state. She signed, the land was sold, and my father was one of eight children who inherited.

When my father died I received my inheritance, part of which was the money from the sale of Mr. Poole's land. For a long time I pondered what to do. I did not feel like I could accept money I had witnessed my grandfather refuse on the afternoon on the back porch so many years before. So I waited. I did nothing. I never spent one dime of that money.

In 2016 an idea came to me that seemed an appropriate way to use that money. It is the money being used to produce the Expository Series. I did not know of any Apostolic writings that were doing an Expository Series. So I took that money and began to print books for Apostolic people to read.

The books of the Expository Series are printed without charge to the authors. The proceeds and profit of the books sold online go back into a non-profit fund to print more Apostolic books. None of the online profit is going to any personal use for anyone. If an author buys his book direct from wholesale after it is published and sells it, then he is welcomed to keep any profit from those sales.

I would like to thank all the men who have contributed their work to this endeavor. Scott Hall, Bart Adkins, Vaughn Reece, Kevin Archer, Ben Weeks, and Edward Seabrooks have all contributed. We have now published fifteen volumes and have three more to be published in the next sixty days. Others have also shown interest in publishing their works. Our goal is to have twenty volumes published by the end of 2017.

The publisher we are using has informed me we are their best seller they have ever published. We have now sold several thousand dollars of books since September 1, 2016. I am deeply grateful to everyone who has purchased our product.

Now you know the story behind the Expository Series. A simple Christian man with ethics and morals, opened his heart, and showed me his faith on a warm spring day, in a simple homestead, many years ago. Today I say thank you to my grandfather, Millard Deramus. Thank you for your ethics. Thank you for your morals. Thank you for your Christian faith.

May your memory be blessed and revered. You never

travelled 100 miles from where you were born, but your legacy has spanned America.

www.ingramcontent.com/pod-product-compliance
Lightning Source LLC
Chambersburg PA
CBHW040418100526
44588CB00022B/2866